Effective Employee Training

Steven M. Bragg

AccountingTools®

ISBN 978-1-64221-191-7

For more information about AccountingTools® products, visit our Web site at www.accountingtools.com.

Table of Contents

About the Author

Steven Bragg, CPA, has been the chief financial officer or controller of four companies, as well as a consulting manager at Ernst & Young. He received a master's degree in finance from Bentley College, an MBA from Babson College, and a Bachelor's degree in Economics from the University of Maine. He has been a two-time president of the Colorado Mountain Club, and is an avid alpine skier, mountain biker, and certified master diver. Mr. Bragg resides in Centennial, Colorado. He has written more than 300 books and courses, including *New Controller Guidebook*, *GAAP Guidebook*, and *Payroll Management*.

Steven maintains the accountingtools.com web site, which contains continuing professional education courses, the Accounting Best Practices podcast, and thousands of articles on accounting subjects.

Chapter 1
Overview of Training

Introduction

The point behind training employees is to improve the performance of the organization. This is especially critical when a company is constantly reinventing itself, either to increase its market share or simply to keep up with the competition. To this end, management pours money into training employees, hoping that doing so will make the organization more nimble, innovative, service oriented, and so forth. In many (if not most) cases, training does not result in such a performance boost – instead, employees soon revert to their old ways, ignoring what they have been taught. The underlying problem is that the organization must be properly designed to support training, so that employees are encouraged to implement what they have learned.

In this chapter, we present an overview of the issues related to training and the administrative aspects of running a training program, before diving into the details of producing the program in the following chapters.

Reasons for Training

There are multiple reasons why a business would want its employees to engage in training. Consider the following:

- *Skill gaps*. There are clear gaps between the current skill sets of employees and what they are expected to need in the future.
- *Consistency*. A key element in building a corporate culture is to ensure that all employees are taught the same company values and policies.
- *Competitive pressures*. When a competitor introduces a new process, product, distribution channel or other innovation, the company may need to react by quickly training up its own staff to match the actions of the competitor.
- *Position requirements*. When employees are being groomed for advancement or for lateral shifts across the organization, this frequently calls for additional training to fill the needs of the new positions being filled. For example, they may need to learn different work habits and social skills when they move into a management position.
- *Efficiency improvements*. When there is a need to improve the efficiency of a process, technical training in targeted areas may be needed. For example, employees could be trained in how to improve the efficiency of equipment changeovers for a new job.
- *Employee retention*. When employees are considered unusually valuable, training can be used as a targeted benefit to keep them from leaving the firm.

- *New product development.* Employee skills in the product development arena can be enhanced so that they have a better knowledge of how to create better products, and to do so with a reduced cycle time. Training can be used to improve their knowledge of framing problems, choosing ideas, testing proto-types, and so forth.

Though there are many reasons to engage in training, the essential focus is on improving business performance. An organization is constantly improving as a result of its training initiatives. When performance improves, it is easy to justify a training program.

Reasons Why Training Fails

The many reasons just enumerated for having training should drive a business to have a highly effective training program – and yet this is rarely the case. Instead, businesses pour money into training endeavors and then experience minimal improvements in their performance. Why? The following issues all have an impact:

- *Lack of a baseline.* Many organizations do not have a clear understanding of the skills that their employees already have. The result is training programs that are too elementary or too advanced for the workforce. The result is minimal absorption of new concepts.
- *Lack of tailoring.* Many training programs are not designed to the specific needs of a business. Instead, they cover general topics that may be of modest interest to participants, but which do little to address the actual needs of the organization.
- *Lack of oversight.* Management may be signing off on training expenditures without paying attention to the types of training and how it is being supported within the organization. Instead, they simply treat the expenditure as another line item on the income statement to be approved.
- *Too much content.* A certain amount of time is required to effectively transmit information. If the trainer attempts to jam too much information into a training session, there is a risk that little or none of the information will be retained.
- *Entrenched methods.* When employees return from a training class, full of nifty new ideas, they find that the department's processes are entrenched in the old manner of doing things. Unless they are strongly supported by management, employees will find that they have little power to change the established system, and find it easier to return to their accustomed routines.
- *Lack of strategic clarity.* The management team may have set forth an unco-ordinated set of goals and values. As a result, employees do not understand what is expected of them, and so do not take action to implement what they have learned.
- *Top-down style of management.* When decisions are being imposed from above, it is more likely that employees will follow the lead set by senior

management, rather than trying out the new perspectives offered during training classes.

- *Cross-functional conflict.* Changes resulting from training frequently require the cooperation of multiple departments, so if one department manager refuses to cooperate, then an improvement project will not proceed.
- *Lack of upward knowledge transfer.* Employees may not be willing to inform management about the reasons for training failures.

When one or more of the preceding issues are causing training initiatives to fail, employees become increasingly cynical about the need for training, even though the managers imposing training are still enthusiastic about it. There are several reasons for this disparity. First, the human resources department has an interest in recommending training programs to support corporate strategies, since this department is responsible for training programs within the organization. And second, it can be difficult to measure the effectiveness of training programs, so that the employees spending so much of their time in training programs are aware of their lack of success, but this information never works its way back up to senior management through its standard set of reporting metrics. These issues mean that a company may keep spending money on training, even though the expenditures have little impact on company performance.

Training Strategy

The best return on investment occurs when training expenditures are closely aligned with an organization's strategy. When this is the case, training is a derivation of the direction in which a business wants to go, rather than being a standard set of training sessions that do not vary much over time. It also means that training is more likely to be custom-designed for the specific needs of the firm, rather than being the usual mix of outside training classes, seminars, and degree programs.

When training is used to directly support strategy, the training cost can vary markedly from year to year, depending on the need for it in the strategic planning documents. For example, if the business is re-orienting itself into a new market, this may call for a massive training effort to familiarize many employees with the requirements of that new market. Conversely, if a spin-off is planned in order to shrink the business, there may be only a minimal return on investment associated with training.

A fully-developed linkage between strategy and training mandates that training needs to be itemized at the level of the individual employee, where each individual is given a personalized development plan. Doing so ensures that each person sees the linkage between his or her training plan and the direction of the entire business, which contributes to a sense of involvement with and support for the business.

The Role of the Training Department

Traditionally, the training department has developed a standard set of training classes, which it conducts on a regular basis. In essence, it develops a set of training products, and then works on efficiently delivering the training materials. While this approach may be efficient, it is not in any way effective. The only effective training occurs when the business outcome is defined in advance of the training, so that the training is designed for a specific need, and then employees are supported all the way through their implementation of the learned concepts. Thus, effective training spans a much broader range of activities, and results in different training materials, than would be the case with the traditional efficient training department.

In its role as an effective organization, the training department acts as a supporting partner to the other departments, attending strategy sessions and polling the department managers about their needs. The result is constant communication with department managers about a series of training initiatives, ranging from those being contemplated for future action to other training sessions conducted months ago, for which implementation efforts are still ongoing. In this role, the training department is an integral part of the daily activities of a business.

Motivations for Training

Employees should not feel that the time allocated to training activities is a burden. Instead, they should be focused forcefully on the need to engage in training. There are several ways to motivate employees. First, raise performance expectations, so that it is more difficult to attain the highest performance ratings. Employees will then realize that only by engaging in ongoing training activities can they hope to attain the highest ratings, which is linked to higher compensation. Second, minimize the linkage between seniority and compensation, emphasizing that compensation will instead be based on critical skills and exceptional performance. Doing so shifts a large part of the compensation budget into the hands of those employees who have engaged in training.

Training Measurements

Training is one of the more difficult parts of a business to measure, since it is designed to impart skills which are used at a later date to improve the organization. This delay between training and any measurable outcome introduces the possibility that other issues have played a role in corporate improvements, thereby making the effects of training less quantifiable. Nonetheless, there are several ways to measure training, as noted in the following bullet points:

- *Post-completion surveys*. By issuing a survey immediately after training has been completed, one can collect employee impressions about what worked well and not so well during a training session. This information can then be used to iteratively improve the training.
- *Test scores during and after training*. One can test employee knowledge both before and after training, to see if a course improved their knowledge of the subject matter. However, this testing does not account for any subsequent decline in knowledge retention.
- *Percentage of employees who achieve acceptable improvement*. This measure focuses on how many employees experience an increase in their performance

up to a predetermined threshold level as the result of a training session. This is a good indicator of knowledge transfer into the workplace.

- *Influence on key performance indicators*. Look for a demonstrable improvement in key business metrics, such as sales, gross margins, and first time quality.
- *Influence on incidents*. This measure looks at declines in key incidents, such as safety problems, lawsuits, or regulatory citations.
- *Informal manager feedback*. This approach is a search for opinions, such as whether an employee is observed to have a better sales technique; though not precise, it can still provide feedback about the possible efficacy of training.
- *Employee retention*. It is less expensive to retain existing employees than to hire new ones, so the impact of training on lowering employee turnover rates should certainly be tracked. However, there may not be a direct linkage between training and turnover.
- *Customer satisfaction survey*. Poll customers to see if they feel there have been changes in employee performance after they attended training. Many factors can influence customer satisfaction, however, so an altered polling result may be difficult to trace back to a training class.
- *Unused learning*. This is the amount of time and money spent on training that was not translated into improved corporate performance. It is difficult to arrive at a quantitative measure, but the concept can be used to make management aware of situations in which the bulk of the resources spent on training are wasted – doing so can trigger a renewed focus on the implementation of learned skills.

A particular emphasis should be placed on the return on investment (ROI) associated with training. A training expenditure should not be considered a discretionary expense that could have been withheld in order to increase profits. Instead, there should be a projected savings or increase in revenues associated with the training, which can then be compared to the training investment. For example, a training class on phone sales costs $1,000, but causes attendees to increase their annual sales by $20,000. Or, a training class on process efficiencies costs $2,500, but leads to the halving of the equipment setup time for a key piece of production equipment, triggering $20,000 of additional profits from being able to produce more goods per year.

The return on investment concept can be used to develop a sorted listed of possible training classes, where some classes generate a higher return than others. If so, management can certainly assign a higher priority to making investments in the higher-ROI training, though some low-ROI classes may involve safety, regulatory, or other similar topics that do not necessarily have a glittering return, but which are essential to the operations of the business.

Another way to allocate investments in training classes is to direct the largest amount of resources towards training initiatives that support the most strategically important parts of the business, even if the projected return on investment is not that high. This approach assumes that there will eventually be a significant payoff from these areas of the business. Conversely, those parts of the business considered to be strategically unimportant and possibly ripe for divestment receive only a minimal investment in training funds.

A variation on the ROI concept can be used by businesses in financial distress. These organizations may be more interested in earning a quick payback on their funds in order to maintain their short-term cash flows. If so, it may be more important to calculate the payback period, which is the amount invested divided by the annual cash flows expected as a result of the training. A firm in financial distress is more likely to pursue training opportunities that have payback periods of just a few months.

> **Tip:** Be sure to share ROI and payback results with the company controller or CFO, since they are familiar with these concepts and can provide significant support for more training – if the measurements have sufficiently favorable results.

Summary

An essential concept in training is that the training given must align with the needs of the organization. Thus, the type and quantity of training given is derived from the overall strategy and supporting tactics employed by a business. When the strategy or tactics change, then so too must the training plan.

Chapter 2
Instructional Systems Design

Introduction

The trouble with training is that merely dumping information on employees does not necessarily mean that they will retain the knowledge. Instead, the information needs to be collected, reformulated, and presented in such a manner that employees will absorb and use it. In addition, there must be a support structure in place, so that employees will be fully assisted in how they implement what they have learned. In this chapter, we describe how the training cycle and its component parts can be used to develop an effective training program.

The Training Cycle

A business should have a standard methodology for developing training materials, so that its training is most effective in meeting the needs of its employees. A common sequence of activities is as follows:

1. *Analyze*. This is an initial assessment to identify the specific needs of employees, which may include interviews to identify their existing experience and expertise. This assessment may find that the needs of employees can be met by means other than training, such as the use of coaching or references to readily available on-line information. If training *is* needed, the analysis results in a set of training objectives – what needs to be taught. Analysis can involve the use of questionnaires, personal interviews, observation of people at work, or the review of existing reports.

2. *Design*. This is a statement of exactly what the planned training should accomplish. The result could be a statement of the performance an employee should exhibit once the training has been completed, or a statement of what the trainer expects to accomplish, or both. There should be a clear definition of exactly what on-the-job performance improvement is expected to happen as a result of the training.

3. *Develop*. This step requires the detailed formulation of training materials, which may be printed or on-line, or in audio or video formats. The development phase includes the creation of instructor materials. The trainer may also choose to pre-test the materials with a pilot training group, which can offer feedback on how to improve the training program.

4. *Implement*. This step involves conducting training sessions. When doing so, the instructor should read the audience to see how the material is being received, and adjust the manner of delivery and materials covered if doing so better meets their needs.

5. *Evaluate*. In this final step, decide whether the original objectives were realized, and whether the training materials and manner of delivery can be

improved upon. One can then decide whether to alter the program for the next batch of employees, and whether the improvements can also be applied to other programs.

Additional comments regarding these activities are included in the following sub-sections.

Analysis and Design

The single most essential element of the training cycle is buried within the analysis and design activities, where a solid business case must be built for conducting training. If there is no clear-cut business case, then even the best-designed and most perfectly-delivered training will not be effective in delivering usable results for a business.

It can be difficult for managers to develop a business case for training. They may simply assume that training needs to accompany a new initiative, such as "there are too many mistakes in order fulfillment, so we need to retrain the staff." The search for a business case may require some questioning, such as:

What is the gap between our current error level and where it needs to be?

What is the current error level costing the company?

Can you talk about the specific types of improvement we need in this area?

Where is the process failing us?

What behavior change are you looking for?

The questioning needs to continue until the person asking for training has a clear picture of how training will improve his area of responsibility in a measurable way.

Development

When developing a training program, it can be useful for the trainer to view every aspect of the presentation from the perspective of the person attending the class. Consider such factors as the level of the person's training and experience, and his prior experience with the company's training program. By doing so, the trainer should be able to address the following questions on behalf of the attendees:

- Will this training be useful for me? Is it worth attending?
- Will I be bored? Will the course material be too difficult for me?
- Do I understand how this training relates to my work?
- In what ways will I be able to incorporate these concepts into my work?

An issue to be aware of when creating training materials is that the human brain can only handle a few chunks of information at a time – typically in the range of two to four items. So if the training materials try to jam in additional information, some portion of it will not be retained. To work around this issue, the training materials need to incorporate additional techniques to assist in the learning process. For example, the materials can employ different presentation techniques to grab an employee's attention, such as a relevant chart, or a brief audio or video segment, or perhaps the use of questions or brief case studies interspersed throughout the text. Another option is to narrowly focus the training on a specific topic to ensure that the recipient has the maximum opportunity to absorb the information – and then take a break to create separation from the next topic.

Implementation

When conducting a training session, it is critical to grab the attention of the attendees at once. Otherwise, their attention will be difficult to regain later in the training session. Do something unexpected to gain their attention, such as playing a quirky video, conducting a demonstration, or giving a quiz. Once their attention has been gained, clarify what the class offers that will help them. Doing so solidifies their interest in the training. Then ascertain their prior knowledge in the subject area, and present the new information in such a manner that it builds on what they already know. Address the subject matter from several directions in order to help them store the material in long-term memory, such as through group discussions, quizzes, breakout sessions, and practice. Practice is especially helpful, so provide it in multiple forms, such as via role playing and problems to be solved. Through these steps, the trainer provides employees with constant feedback, to reinforce what they are learning.

> **Tip:** The attention of participants can begin to wander after as little as 10 minutes, so try to break training concepts down into chunks of no more than 10 minutes, with breaks for stories, exercises, videos, and so forth.

Evaluation

It can be useful to prolong the evaluation phase, to see if the topics included in the training session have actually been implemented on the job. Waiting for clear results provides the best input regarding the effectiveness of the training. However, one should also use early indicators of success to see if there is any positive outcome being derived from training; otherwise, waiting a long time for a clear indication of success could raise the question of whether other factors besides training have also had an impact on the measured outcome.

EXAMPLE

The business purpose behind a training initiative is to increase the rate at which minorities are promoted into management, by improving their management skills. However, it may take several years before there is a clear trend in this direction. To gain an early indication of the success of the training, the company can use 360-degree feedback to see if there is any indication of improvement in the targeted group.

The form of measurement used to decide whether training has been effective should be defined by the person sponsoring the training, not the training department. The sponsor is presumably paying for the training out of his or her budget, and so is the only person who can decide whether the training was worth the investment. This measurement should be agreed upon during the analysis and design phases of the training cycle, since the definition of this measurement has a large impact on the design of the training materials.

Additional Thoughts

These activities are conducted in a loop, where the initial evaluation of a training program is used to initiate the next iteration of the program, thereby increasing its effectiveness over time. Items that may be adjusted in later iterations include the delivery method, the course content, the course objectives, and even the target group to be trained.

The Training Delivery Method

Training can be delivered in many ways. Much of the discussion about training tends to concentrate on formal training programs (which is the main focus of this manual), but only a small portion of the total employee learning experience is based on these programs. The bulk of all employee learning actually comes from social interactions with others and on-the-job activities. A sampling of these training delivery methods are noted in the following bullet points.

Formal training programs

- Apprenticeships
- Certification programs
- College classes
- On-site classroom
- Self-paced e-learning
- Self-study
- Virtual classroom

Learning from others

- Coaching
- Conducting research
- Mentoring
- Networking
- Peer feedback

<u>On-the-job activities</u>

- Engaging in rotational assignments
- Installing new systems
- Managing change activities
- Resolving problems
- Taking on stretch assignments

The ideal training program that yields the best results will probably require a blended approach that incorporates all three of the preceding classifications of training delivery methods. For example, a collections manager wants to train his staff in skip tracing[1] techniques. He begins with a formal classroom session to introduce the basic skip tracing concepts, which is followed immediately by one-on-one coaching by a skip tracing expert. In addition, each collections person is assigned a difficult skip tracing assignment, with the work being monitored by a qualified skip tracing expert. This comprehensive approach to training is much more likely to result in collections people who are now comfortable with using skip tracing to track down delinquent customers.

> **Tip:** The key point when selecting a training delivery method, as well as the content of the training, is to use whatever combination of techniques is most applicable, based on the topic, the audience, and the information to be imparted.

Within just the formal training program classification, the delivery method chosen can depend on a number of factors. For example, if only a few employees will be available at any given time, then a self-study solution may work best. Conversely, if the training must be completed within a short period of time, an on-site or virtual classroom can be used to run a number of people through the program. As another example, if the knowledge to be imparted is highly technical or new to employees, an on-site classroom may be best, since there will be a teacher present who can work with employees as needed. Yet another common situation is for employees to be located in different offices, in which case a virtual classroom may be the best solution.

E-learning solutions can represent a significant improvement in the efficiency of delivering information to employees. By using e-learning, one can avoid all travel costs, since the training is delivered at an employee's desk. Also, the bulk cost of e-learning tends to be quite low, so a company that needs to train a large number of employees could cost-effectively do so through an e-learning platform. Further, many e-learning systems allow a user to pause the instruction and return to it later, or at least divides the content into small, manageable chunks. And finally, employees can access e-learning training classes at any time of the day, making it more convenient to take classes.

---

[1] The process of locating a person's whereabouts

The Positive Impact of a Program's Description

Employees are more likely to want to attend a training session when it has been described to them in terms of its benefits. Employees want to attend training when it promises to yield a practical benefit for them, such as a more efficient way to conduct their work. However, trainers tend to write course descriptions based on the topics that will be covered, rather than the benefits to be gained. While topics are interesting, they do not sell a training session to an employee, so the person is less likely to be actively engaged in the training.

EXAMPLE

A training department sponsors a training class for credit analysts that describes the course as follows:

> During the training session, we will cover the construction of credit scoring models, credit policy optimization, and the use of solvency ratio analysis.

An employee would have a hard time extracting any benefits from this laundry list of training features. A revised course description that focuses on benefits might read as follows:

> This class teaches you how to spot dodgy credit applications and minimize bad debt losses. Bring recent examples of bad debt losses, and we will discuss how you could have spotted them in advance.

The Need for Pre-Work

It may be necessary to assign work to attendees prior to the start of a training session. The intent is to establish a common base of knowledge among the participants, so that the trainer does not have to spend time educating anyone during the training session whose knowledge is below the minimum required for the course. When everyone enters a training session with a common knowledge base, they will be better able to understand the relevance of what they are being taught, and will be more effective in group interaction.

Learning Activities

The exact structure of a training session can vary substantially by organization, and even from class to class. Nonetheless, it can be useful to follow a standard progression within a class in order to maximize the amount of learning achieved. For example, a training session could be structured around the following activities:

1. *Gain the employee's attention.* First impressions are critical, so consider introducing an unusual element into the beginning of the class, perhaps using unusual props or an interesting story.

2. *Discuss the training objectives.* By discussing objectives, employees will realize why something is important and how it will affect them, and so will be more inclined to invest in the required learning activity.

3. *Discuss any prior learning by employees in the same area.* Talking about the prior learning or related experiences of attendees allows the trainer to focus on those areas that will build upon what they already know.

4. *Engage in the training session.* The training session uses multiple approaches to the presentation and discussion of information to enhance knowledge retention.

5. *Include a knowledge practice session.* This could be a discussion of how the new knowledge may be applied to the specific circumstances of each employee, or how it connects to other ideas they are considering, or even discussing the weaknesses in the new information, or what types of additional information is needed to round out the topic.

6. *Ask for feedback.* Any information garnered from attendees can be used to enhance the next iteration of the training class.

All of the preceding activities are designed to engage the employee, so that the person is more fully centered on the information being imparted. Ideally, the best information retention occurs when employees have the opportunity to see the training materials, discuss them, and then do them. Otherwise, the level of learning tends to be superficial, with people only remembering a few percent of the training materials.

Tip: Employees become more invested in training when they perceive it to be highly practical. Thus, information about a theoretical topic will not be retained unless it is accompanied by a large proportion of practical usage topics.

A further retention technique is to create a system under which employees learn the material and then become the trainers for other employees. When employees know that they must be the trainer in the immediate future, they are much more inclined to retain information.

Changes to the Training

The trainer may inquire as to the expectations of participants regarding what they would like to get out of the training class. What should the trainer do if these expectations differ from what is included in the training materials? Here are several possible courses of action:

- Lengthen the training period to include the additional topics.
- Ask participants if there are any topics that can be removed from the agenda, to be replaced by the new topics.
- See if the additional expectations only apply to a few people; if so, ask them to meet afterwards or at a different time to go over the new topics.

- State that those topics can be addressed in a different training session, with an offer to conduct the training at a later date.
- Offer to send them relevant training materials after the training session has been concluded.

It is useful to work with participants in this manner, since they will then be more likely to buy into the training program, knowing that it meshes with their expectations.

Learning Objectives

The starting point of a training class is a set of learning objectives. These objectives should specify the desired knowledge or skill of the employee after training has been completed. More specifically, an ideal learning objective should be highly specific, relevant to the training needs of the organization, and measurable. An objective is measurable when one can clearly state whether it has been completed at the end of a training session. Several examples of learning objectives are:

You will be able to close the accounts payable module at month-end.

You will be able to walk through the steps needed to complete the monthly sales tax remittance form.

You will be able to derecognize fixed assets from the accounting records when assets are dispositioned.

Objectives are needed for an effective training program, so that employees have a clear understanding of what they are supposed to be learning. Also, having a clear set of objectives makes it easier for the trainer to develop targeted course materials; otherwise, there is a risk that stray topics will be included that are not relevant and waste the time of both the trainer and the attending employees. A clear set of objectives can also be used as the basis for an evaluation of the training materials and the trainer, since employees can compare the list of objectives to what they were taught. An added bonus is when the trainer can show employees how the objectives relate back to their jobs and (better yet) specific issues they are facing.

The Spacing Effect

The human brain can only absorb a certain amount of information within a block of time. If the trainer attempts to jam in additional information during this time slot, employees will not retain the information, because their ability to remember is overloaded. In addition, people have difficulty absorbing information if they are exposed to it just once. Conversely, the absorption of information is enhanced by spreading out training sessions and covering the same material multiple times during these sessions. This effect is called the *spacing effect*.

There are several ways to structure a training program to take advantage of the spacing effect. One possibility is to teach a series of truncated training sessions, with each one covering the minimum amount of time needed to impart the essential knowledge. Another option is to alter the form of training in each session; for example, the first session is a lecture, the second session is a video presentation, and the third session involves a hands-on case study. Yet another variation is to have a discussion session about the topic. It is quite possible to combine these alternatives to maximize the learning experience over a series of training sessions.

The Negative Effects of Too Much Information

It is quite easy for a trainer to stuff too much information into a training class. When this happens, an informational fire hose is being turned on the participants, who cannot begin to assimilate everything. When too much information is presented, employees do not even learn the basic concepts, since they have no time to process what they have learned, and so do not understand how the various concepts interact.

One way to get around the problem of providing too much information is to initially structure a training session with just the basic concepts, supported by all applicable discussion, practice, and other activities meant to reinforce the basic concepts. Conduct a pilot training session with just these concepts, and time its duration. Then incrementally add more material to fill up the allocated training period, but only if the additional material directly relates to the core concepts. This approach is easier than starting with an overstuffed training regimen and then having to pare it down to the designated training period.

> **Tip:** Even when the amount of information included in a training session is reasonable, participants can feel overwhelmed if the trainer talks too fast. Thus, slowing down one's speaking speed can have a notable positive impact on the learning of employees.

A variation on the concept is to only structure a training session around what employees need to know in order to perform better on the job, with all other information stripped out. Viewing the training from this perspective allows for the elimination of many "nice to know" but ultimately not usable details, such as who developed a theory or how the theory has been modified by subsequent researchers.

The Need for Visuals

Employee knowledge retention improves when the standard training session is supplemented with visuals. By doing so, a participant may grasp a training concept quicker and understand it better. This is because visuals can convey information quickly and succinctly. In addition, people tend to remember information conveyed through visuals for a longer period of time. This is especially important for people who are new to the training topic, since they might otherwise struggle to understand the underlying concepts.

Some types of visuals work better than others. Consider the following improvement possibilities:

- *Simplicity*. A simplified visual is easier to understand. It is especially difficult for a person to read a complex slide while listening to the trainer at the same time. Therefore, avoid visuals that are crammed with information; it may be possible to split these visuals into several simplified visuals.
- *Tied to complex topics*. Visuals are most useful when they are tied to complex topics that are difficult to understand. Conversely, there is less need for visuals when the underlying topic is a simple one.
- *Supported by commentary*. When displaying a visual, always describe its contents; this auditory support confirms the information being presented, and may be useful when the visual is not entirely clear.
- *New graphics*. Users are accustomed to (and bored by) the standard PowerPoint presentation. To grab their attention, try some variations on the standard presentation, such as an altered color scheme, different bullet points, or an unusual font. However, the changes cannot distract from the underlying message.

The preceding points are primarily targeted at PowerPoint visuals. One might be tempted to also include videos in the presentation. If so, use them with care, since they may move well away from the main message of the presentation. Videos work best when they are targeted at the demonstration of a specific skill or to illustrate a certain kind of behavior.

Flipcharts can be a useful visual when they are created during a training session. They can be used to create lists that are contributed by participants, or to compile ideas put forward by the group. As such, they bolster the level of participation by employees in training.

The Need for Stories

An employee will find it quite difficult to extract anything meaningful from the dry recitation of facts. After a while, a person can be expected to blank out and let any additional information wash over him, untouched. A better way to grab someone's attention is to insert stories into the training. A well-told story can strongly reinforce a key point in the training, and also represents a welcome break from what might otherwise be a monotonous training session. A variation on the concept is to tell part of a story, and then finish the story later in the presentation.

The Need for Participant Practice

An employee is much more likely to retain a new concept if it can be reinforced with practice. To optimize the amount of information retention, avoid simply repeating information in a practice session. Instead, conduct practice sessions within the context of real-world scenarios, so that participants can see how concepts can be applied within their work environments.

The amount of practice incorporated into a training session depends on the circumstances. For example, if a person will be able to use a cheat sheet on the job to follow a series of work steps, then practice is less necessary, since there are fewer consequences to not having memorized the relevant information. Conversely, if the consequences of an on-the-job error are serious and using a cheat sheet is not an option, then it is much more important to engage in practice sessions.

Practice sessions should be sprinkled throughout the learning experience, rather than being aggregated into a single large practice session at the end of the training. By using short practice sessions at measured intervals, employees can work with smaller amounts of information at a time, allowing them to better absorb the information. Later in the training, several training concepts can be combined into a more complex practice session, where participants can meld several learning modules into a real-world case study.

Try to make practice sessions as realistic as possible. This could involve the use of a case study that mimics an actual event, such as a fraud investigation, the setup of a machine that is actually used in the production process, or taking a customer order over the phone, using a recording of an actual conversation with a customer.

Once a practice session has been completed, be sure to give feedback on how well someone has performed, noting positive outcomes that should be continued, as well as negative outcomes that should be reduced or avoided. Spotting issues during practice allows the instructor to loop back through concepts that have not been fully absorbed. After such a reiteration, the instructor may elect to conduct the practice session again to ensure that employees understand the concepts, and then move on to the next learning segment.

Tip: Consider overloading on practice sessions, so that participants have enough repetitions to really master the skills being taught. However, doing so will restrict the number of topics that can be covered.

The Need for Novelty

The brain tends to remember information that is associated with novel occurrences. If those novel occurrences are repeated, however, the brain becomes habituated to them and so is less likely to remember any associated information. This concept can be applied to the design of instructional systems. For example, the trainer can introduce an unusual prop at some point during the training, such as a humorous picture, or shift his location to start teaching from the middle of the classroom, or hand out jelly beans for a mid-morning snack. Or, serve popcorn when a video is being shown. The main point is that the introduction of unique events can be used to improve the retention of information.

When to Provide Performance Support

There are times when relying on the memorization of information is not sufficient, where flowcharts, templates, checklists, and similar tools are needed to ensure that the best outcome is achieved. The intent behind using these tools is to show the best way to execute procedures or apply learning. These types of performance support are most necessary under the following circumstances:

- When an error would be costly or dangerous
- When procedures change frequently
- When the task to be performed is quite complex
- When a procedure will only be performed at long intervals

In these situations, it makes sense to support the long-term performance of employees by providing them with additional tools, such as:

- *Calendar*. States the dates and times when activities must be initiated.
- *Checklists*. Ensures that the most critical and important activities are completed.
- *Decision trees*. Shows the decision points in a logical flow of activities.
- *Flow charts*. Visually presents the flow of a process.
- *Searchable information database*. Provides access to a large body of knowledge.
- *Step-by-step instructions*. Ensures that the correct sequence of steps is followed.
- *Videos*. Shows exactly how to perform a procedure.
- *Worksheet*. Ensures that all steps in a calculation are completed.

Whatever the tool may be, it is essential that it be readily available for use at the point when the related task is performed. Otherwise, an employee is much less likely to spend the extra time to find and use the tool. For example, instructions for how to open a tool chest should be affixed to the tool chest, not stashed away in an on-line database.

A benefit of providing performance support is that it can replace training entirely, or at least only requires modest training in how to access and use the support tools. Further, performance support tools are typically less-expensive to design than training materials, and can be revised at low cost.

Tip: The best performance support is embedded in the process where it is needed, so that only the most relevant information is right there, readily accessible to the user.

Performance support tools work best when they are introduced and used during training. Some tools may be considered so critical that they are the central point of the training, with the rest of the instruction built around how to use the tools. Then, when employees return to work, they can bring the tools along with them and immediately begin using them.

Methods of Evaluation

How is it possible to tell if training has been effective? There are several levels of evaluation questions that can be used, ranging from the initial reaction of employees to the training, all the way to the results experienced by the business. The full range of possible evaluations is:

1. *Reaction to the training.* At this lowest level of evaluation response, the trainer simply asks if the training has met the expectations of the participants. For example, the trainer might ask if employees believe the training to have been relevant to their work. At this level, the question is simple and takes little time to collect information. However, the survey is being taken at the point when participants have full memory of what they have learned – this amount will decline significantly after the training has been completed. This is also not a good predictor of future changes in employee performance.

2. *Skills learned.* This evaluation tests participants to see how much knowledge has initially been retained. For example, the trainer could ask employees to define the range of actions that can be taken to defuse a tense situation. This questioning takes more time, but information can be collected right away, at the end of the training session. This approach can be limited to testing the factual recall of information, so it may not adequately reflect the long-term impact of the training.

3. *Behavior changes.* This evaluation tests whether the training has resulted in behavioral changes, such as altering one's approach to a personal interaction or a more efficient way to handle a task. For example, the trainer could follow up with employees and their managers to see if they have implemented a faster closing process in the accounting department. The information collected may include measurements related to changes in process efficiencies, cost reductions, and revenue increases. This evaluation takes much more time to collect, and there may be a significant delay before it can be collected.

4. *Business results.* This evaluation quantifies the results caused by the training, such as a reduction in expenses. There may be operational improvements as well, such as changes in the number of customer complaints, product defects, and safety violations. For example, one might measure the before-and-after cost of placing an order with a supplier. There can be a delay of several months in collecting this information, depending on the data collection capabilities of the business.

When a significant amount is being invested in training, one would certainly want to engage in the most detailed form of evaluation (business results). Conversely, lower-cost, short-duration training sessions may not be worth the extensive effort required to derive business results, so perhaps a simple collection of reactions to the training would be sufficient. For more measurement options, see the Training Measurements section in the first chapter.

The Negative Impact of Inadequate Training

One of the drivers of employee behavior in a training class is the reputation of the training program, which is built up within the organization by the quality of its prior training classes. When a trainer delivers a training session that does not address a business purpose, contains inadequate materials, or is poorly executed, employees are more likely to remember the experience than any number of well-constructed and perfectly executed classes. Thus, a small number of training failures can trigger a long-term negative view of the training institution, which means that employees will start training without overly high expectations, and with no burning desire to make use of the resulting information.

There are a few ways to minimize the risk of inadequate training. Pilot testing can be used to spot inadequate training materials or poor instructor performance, especially for newer trainers. The training department can also set minimum standards for how courses are to be structured and formatted. It is also essential to work with sponsoring managers to ensure that there is a clear business purpose behind every training initiative.

There may be cases in which employees are uncomfortable in a classroom setting, perhaps due to bad experiences with such environments at other companies or in school. To avoid this negative association, training sessions can be conducted in the field or in a shop environment, where the focus is on hands-on activities that are more fully engaging than may be the case in a more sterile classroom situation.

The Positive Impact of Management Support

Employees listen carefully to what their managers say, because managers have control over salary increases, promotions, and advancement. Consequently, employees will notice when managers do not actively support a training initiative. Perhaps a manager grouses about an employee being taken away from her tasks for the day to attend a training session, or maybe the manager says nothing at all about an upcoming class. In these situations, the employee assumes that the training is not important, and so shows up with the intention of simply attending the class and then returning to her job, with no intent to implement what she has learned.

The situation is entirely different when the manager is actively supportive. When a manager takes aside an employee and asks her to pay attention in class and bring back ideas to work on, then the employee is much more likely to attend the training with an attentive mindset. Thus, a strong signal from managers that training is important is a key driver of how well employees perform in training.

> **Tip:** Impose a standard policy that all employees scheduled to attend training must first discuss the training with their supervisor. Doing so gives the manager a chance to talk about expectations for the class.

The proper positioning of an employee's mindset going into a training class is critical, since this attitude tends to be self-fulfilling. Thus, a person who greatly anticipates a training session is much more likely to use the resulting information than someone who has minimal expectations for a class.

Management support must continue after a training session has been completed. The manager should meet with everyone returning from a training class to discuss next steps to implement what they have learned, and follow up at regular intervals to check on progress. It is also quite useful for the manager *not* to dump a pile of work on a returning employee, so that there is no time for implementation work; instead, do the reverse and block out enough time for the employee to make the necessary changes. Finally, the manager should create the expectation of some kind of reward that is linked to a proper learning transfer into the workplace, thereby giving the employee an incentive to succeed.

Tip: Consider holding a coaching class for managers *in advance of* any training scheduled for their employees, so that the managers will know how to deal with the employees once they have returned from training. As part of the coaching class, hand out guidelines for post-training actions they should take with employees.

Transferring Training to the Workplace

It can be quite difficult to transfer the knowledge gained in a training session back to the workplace. There are several reasons for this, including training that is not correctly targeted at company problems and the resistance of the organization to change. Another area of concern is that the training department does not take responsibility for the implementation of knowledge, and the departments in which trainees are located do not place a high priority on it. To minimize these issues, it is critical to have a discussion between the trainer and management *prior to* the development of training materials, to talk about the exact needs to be addressed by the training and how management plans to assist with any resulting implementations. For example:

- *Course development.* The group can talk about what employees have to do better for the department to be successful, and the goals to be achieved. The discussion may extend into the particular needs of specific individuals. The outcome is a training program that is specifically targeted at the needs of the business.
- *Management support.* The discussion could revolve around change management – how managers intend to support any new initiatives, break down resistance, and provide an adequate level of support, possibly including incentives. Since this discussion takes place *before* the training, managers are put on alert well in advance that their participation will be needed – and they now have time to plan accordingly.

Managers can also assist with the training effort by meeting with participants in advance to reinforce with them how important it is to fully understand the information being imparted to them during training. Also, if the training requires attendees to read training materials in advance, managers can assist by blocking out sufficient time for them to do so. Another option is for managers to encourage attendees to draw up a list of questions to bring to the training, regarding how they can apply the training to their jobs.

Near the end of a training session, the trainer can build in a discussion about how the employees plan to implement what they have learned. This can be a group discussion, where the participants work together to figure out a plan for how to proceed. By making it a group discussion, the trainer is trying to gain cohesion in the group, so that they will work together during the implementation phase. An essential part of this discussion is to come up with a list of the barriers that will likely be encountered, and how to work around them.

Once training has been completed, participants should meet with their managers at once, to discuss how they can implement what was learned. There should be a series of these meetings, initiated by the manager, to discuss progress and the level of support needed to ensure that the necessary changes are made. If an employee is not in a position where he can immediately make use of his new skills, a possible option is to include him on a cross-functional team or other special project where the skills *can* be used.

Tip: Have training participants prepare periodic progress reports about what they are doing to implement what they have learned in the workplace.

When a manager finds that an employee has persistently *not* been able to implement what he has learned, a reasonable outcome is not to send that person to any additional training, since the company is not achieving any return on its training investment.

Other Training Ideas

The preceding pages have covered the essentials of instructional systems design. In addition, there are many enhancements that can be incorporated into a training program, depending on the circumstances. We have subdivided these best practices into categories, and present them in the following bullet points:

Environmental factors

- *Clearly defined direction.* The management team has developed and thoroughly communicated a well-coordinated strategic direction, which can then be used to develop targeted training.
- *Ability to speak up.* The local manager must have fostered an environment in which employees feel safe in making suggestions. The manager should have established a history of not "dumping cold water" on suggestions, but rather of supporting the exploration of new ideas. Further, if the actions of senior management are causing training initiatives to fail, employees should be able to speak up about these actions without fear of retribution.

Social aspects of training

- *Conduct introductions.* People tend to learn better in a collaborative environment, so block out time at the beginning of training to have each participant talk about themselves and why they are attending the training. Also, when people participate right away, they are more likely to continue doing so throughout the training.
- *Encourage social interaction.* Learning from others is a key part of the overall learning experience. To encourage this type of learning, ask training participants to swap their contact information.
- *Pull aside affected people.* Watch the group during the training session to see if anyone withdraws from the conversation or seems distracted. During breaks, ask them what is the matter, which may present an opportunity to make adjustments to the training or to offer advice.
- *Ban cell phones and laptops.* When training participants try to multi-task by (for example) checking text messages and e-mails during a training session, their performance degrades notably. It is best to ban cell phones and laptops; instead, allow their use only during scheduled breaks.

Specificity of the training

- *Link to personal situation.* Spend time at the beginning of a training session to talk about how the training will have a positive impact on a person's job or life. When an individual sees a clear improvement resulting from the training, he is much more likely to commit quality time to the training.
- *Localize case studies.* When inserting a case study into a training session, try to use an actual situation from within the company, so that employees can see how the training can be used to improve their daily work issues.
- *Solicit problems.* A variation on using local case studies is to ask participants for their own problems that need to be resolved. Doing so proves the efficacy of the training, while also pulling employees into the discussion. A further step is to ask employees prior to the training session to compile a list of questions to bring with them.
- *Application recognition.* Part of the discussion of new skills can be the situations in which they can be applied. This is especially useful when the training materials are more theoretical than practical in nature.
- *Tap into expertise.* If any of the trainees have an unusually high level of expertise, ask them to relate their own experiences at relevant points in the discussion. To do this, the trainer needs to collect background information from participants either before or during the training session.

Effectiveness of the training

- *Review for extraneous information.* Once the first version of training materials has been completed, review it to see if there is any information in the text that goes beyond the requirements of the training objectives. If so, consider throwing them out. These extra materials take time away from the primary learning objectives, which diffuses the attention of the participants.

- *Make them accountable.* Employees are more likely to retain information if they are told in advance by their managers that they will be held accountable for what they learn.
- *Paraphrase the topic.* Have attendees paraphrase what they have learned during a discussion with someone with whom they are paired. Paraphrasing is a good way to lock concepts into long-term memory by forcing a person to think about the meaning of the material and concentrate on summarizing what he has learned.
- *Introduce errors.* The trainer can deliberately include errors into a training session, and then asks participants to identify them. Doing so increases the interactivity of the training, which aids in retaining knowledge.
- *Add modest stress.* Tell participants that there will be a test at intervals. Doing so introduces a modest amount of stress, making them pay more attention. A modest stress level improves the retention of knowledge, though a higher stress level interferes with retention.
- *Overlay multiple topics.* Though a common best practice is to only train employees on one discrete topic at a time, it may make sense to mix two topics together. This approach works when the two topics are closely interrelated. For example, a warehouse design training class could also address cycle counting[2], since such a counting program is more effective when the warehouse bins are laid out in a logical manner that can be efficiently counted.
- *Include collaboration.* Knowledge retention is higher when people work within teams to complete assigned tasks. Doing so results in the participants discussing the training materials within the group, which enhances retention.
- *Block out extra time.* A training session should include enough time for questions and answers, practice, discussions, and breaks. These additional tasks may significantly extend the baseline time required to simply present the training materials, so be sure to block out sufficient time for a training session. Otherwise, the instructor feels compelled to jam the lecture portion into the available training time, and does so by cutting out the other parts of the training.

Lists during the training

- *Create a book list.* Maintain a board on which employees can post the names of relevant books that might be of use to others in the group.
- *Create a parking lot.* Maintain a board on which participants can add ideas and questions.

---

[2] The process of counting a small block of inventory items each day, so that the entire inventory is counted over a period of time

Follow-up training

- *Create a book club.* Encourage training participants to meet occasionally to recommend books and discuss what they have learned from their readings.
- *Issue additional materials.* The trainer can send a stream of additional information to attendees after the formal training has been concluded. This information may include links to on-line articles, scanned articles, tips, and so forth.

Implementation concepts

- *Discuss implementation barriers.* Have the group discuss barriers to implementing the concepts they have learned in the training session, focusing on ways to break through or sidestep those barriers.
- *Include a manager video.* Near the end of the training session, play a video that features a member of senior management, congratulating employees for completing the training session, but also pointing out that the training cannot go to waste – now they need to implement the new concepts they have learned.
- *Train managers as coaches.* When managers have the appropriate skill set as coaches, their employees receive better support in implementing what they have learned.
- *Schedule a manager-employee meeting.* Set up a meeting with the employee and his or her manager after the training has been completed. The employee should brief the manager on the results of the training, followed by a mutual discussion of how the concepts can be implemented.
- *Form a peer group.* Encourage the employees to form peer groups that continue to meet after the formal training has been completed, with the intent of creating a dynamic that leads to a higher rate of implementation success.
- *Meet with the manager.* After some time has passed, the trainer can schedule a meeting with the manager of each trainee, to discuss how the individual has applied his training. The outcome may be more support from the manager to ensure that training topics are used, or perhaps a commitment for additional training, perhaps of a different type.
- *Provide process support.* If employees want to make process changes as an outcome of their training, provide them with the process analysis support needed to design solutions that are more likely to work.
- *Align compensation with implementation.* Update the performance expectations for employees, so they know that part of their compensation will be based on their ability to implement what they have learned.
- *Award completion certificates after implementation.* No course completion certificate should be issued at the end of the training phase, since no implementation has yet been achieved. Instead, award a certificate after some form of implementation by the employee can be proven.

An essential element of the preceding factors is that the environment in which training is conducted must be adjusted *before* the training. Thus, the business must have a clearly defined direction and the environment must allow employees to speak up. In this environment, the right training programs can be selected and the proper amount of support can be given.

Of the other training ideas just noted, pay particular attention to the activities scheduled *after* the formal training has been completed. An organization that succeeds in transferring new knowledge into improved operations does so by ensuring that there is a long tail on a training program; it may engage in follow-up activities for months after a training class has been completed.

Summary

A training program will be vastly more successful when it is integrated into a follow-up campaign that works to implement the information that has been learned. There should be a formal structure in place for working with trainees for an extended period of time to ensure that a solid business outcome is achieved as the result of a training program. When employees know that they will be expected to perform after a training session has been completed, they will be much less likely to take on the role of a spectator, where they merely show up for a training class.

Unfortunately, a company could have an excellent training department that engages in every possible best practice to deliver targeted training to its employees, and yet still does not deliver notable performance improvements. This problem arises when the organization is excessively hidebound, with no interest in changing its policies and procedures. In this situation, the organization swats down any attempts at implementing change. When there is no demonstrable change arising from a firm's training activities, it is quite likely that the training department will be blamed, even though the underlying issue lies elsewhere within the organization. Consequently, senior management needs to monitor implementation efforts in enough detail and understand why the firm is not generating a return on its training investment. Further, the manager of the training department should be given sufficient authority to work with other department managers on an equal basis to implement training initiatives.

Chapter 3
Training Preparation and Interaction

Introduction

The construction of training materials and how they result in implemented improvements are not the only part of a training environment. In addition, the trainer has to consider the physical environment, the learning environment, and dealing with difficult people. We cover these topics and more in the following pages.

The Physical Environment

An essential element of the learning experience is that the physical environment be conducive to learning. This means that there are no distractions in the room for the employees or the trainer. The trainer may be assigned a room and have no further choice in the matter; however, if it is possible to do so, the following issues should be addressed:

- *Additional rooms*. If the training materials call for a breakout session, be sure to reserve one or more adjacent conference rooms for this purpose.
- *Clutter*. Extra furniture, storage boxes, flip charts, and so forth are a distraction for everyone, so they should be removed from the room.
- *Furniture*. The furniture should not be a distraction. This means the tables should not be worn or dirty, and the chairs should be sufficiently comfortable. A facility that regularly hosts training sessions is more likely to have a range of furniture configurations available.
- *Lighting*. The lighting should be bright, since dim lighting puts people to sleep. Natural lighting is best.
- *Power outlets*. Electrical outlets should be tucked out of the way, with extension cords positioned so that no one will trip over them. Where cords are in the open, be sure to tape them down.
- *Seating*. Different seating arrangements are conducive to different types of learning. For example, a "U" shaped fan arrangement is good for switching from listening to a presentation to practicing in groups, while classroom-style seating works well when there is a standard lecture or video presentation. When group discussions are essential, consider seating everyone around a table.
- *Size*. The room should match the number of attendees and the types of activities that will be conducted within it. If the room is too small, it will feel cramped during the trainer's practice sessions and group exercises, and the room will also become excessively hot in short order. Conversely, a large room dwarfs the number of participants and causes echoes.

- *Walls*. When the trainer wants to post flipchart pages on the walls, it is critical that the room has enough wall space to accommodate the pages. This means few windows (if any), and preferably a hard surface that will hold tape.
- *Windows*. If there are windows, they should have functional blinds, so that the sun can be blocked out of the room. Otherwise, the room temperature will increase and the sun's glare will wash out any projected presentation materials.

Tip: A week prior to the training, verify that the correct room has been reserved. It may have been taken over by someone else or double booked.

It is impossible to walk into a room a few minutes before a training session is scheduled to begin and expect that the room conditions will be perfect. There will likely be several issues that immediately cause distractions, and which will take time to correct – time that could otherwise have been spent on training. The ideal way to avoid this situation is to set up the room the day before and conduct a leisurely walkthrough of the entire training class, to see if any corrections need to be made. This involves sitting where the participants will sit, to verify that the lighting is adequate and that they can see the trainer. Set up flipcharts and practice scribbling on them, tearing them off, and hanging them on the walls. Verify that any markers used are not indelible ink that bleeds through the paper. Test all battery-powered remote controls and laser pointers. Plug in and focus the projector. Also consider taping a positioning square around the projector, so that it can be reset to the correct spot if its position is inadvertently shifted. Further, have the phone number on hand for an assistant who can fix the equipment and correct issues with the room.

There may be times when there is a catastrophic failure, such as a dead projector or a corrupted file that housed a PowerPoint presentation. In these cases, be prepared to go manual, which requires a hard copy of the presentation materials that can be used as notes for a presentation.

The Learning Environment

A training participant is more likely to retain knowledge when he is ensconced in a welcoming and safe environment. To create such an environment, the trainer can engage in the following activities to ease their concerns:

Prior to the training

- E-mail all participants directions to the room, parking instructions, a roster of fellow participants, and the schedule of activities
- Post a sign at the door, stating the name of the training session
- Ensure that complete training materials and writing instruments are available in front of every chair
- Ensure that drinks and snacks are available within the room

At the beginning of training

- Greet everyone at the door
- Hand out name placards
- Learn the name of every participant
- Point out that anyone can get up whenever they want, to get more comfortable
- Go over the agenda, so they know what to expect

During the training

- Call on people by name
- Pull people into the conversation at regular intervals
- Use breakout sessions to encourage people to talk
- Allow for differences of opinion
- Be available during breaks and after the training to discuss any issues that people want to bring up

The trainer should place a particular emphasis on the activities noted at the *beginning* of a training session, so that participants are immediately put at their ease when they walk into the room. Doing so sets the tone for the entire day.

We have just noted the many ways in which the instructor can achieve a welcoming and safe environment for trainees. These can all be counterbalanced by a trainer who comes across as cold or detached. This situation is quite common when the trainer wants to appear credible, and so uses an excessively professorial, detached approach. A better way to deal with the situation is to do whatever it takes to appear as approachable as possible, perhaps with some self-deprecating humor or by showing a strong interest in the ideas and perspectives of participants.

The energy level in the room is largely driven by the instructor. The instructor needs to be a "ball of energy" throughout the training, which heightens the activity level in the room. A demonstrated level of enthusiasm for the course materials is an essential element of being a trainer. If the trainer is instead lethargic, be assured that the energy of the entire group will be dragged down.

The Training Materials

At a minimum, the training materials should not interfere with a training session; they should support the concepts being taught, and not distract the attention of participants. Consider taking the following steps to keep the materials from being a distraction:

- Have a third party proof the training materials before they are finalized
- Insert proofed training materials into binders and verify a few binders at random
- If training materials have been delivered from a printing firm, verify a few at random, and with enough time to make corrections
- Create a packing list of every item that will be needed for the training session (see the following exhibit)

Sample Packing List for a Training Session

Batteries	Extension cords	Pens for trainees
Duct tape	Laser pointer	Projector bulb
Emergency phone numbers	Marker pens	Remote controls
	Paper for trainees	

The Training Delivery

A great deal of effort is needed to ensure that the trainer teaches the materials correctly. The trainer will certainly have to run through the materials multiple times in advance, before arriving at the right set of materials, pacing, pauses, and so forth. The following actions are recommended for arriving at a high-quality presentation:

- Practice all stories to be told to ensure that the pacing and punchlines are correct
- Practice all words or phrases that involve difficult enunciation
- Practice in the room to be used for the actual training session
- Ruminate over the types of questions that may be asked by participants
- Record the presentation and critically review it

By practicing in advance, it is easier to display confidence during training sessions, and enthusiasm for the training materials.

> **Tip:** During the practice sessions, make a point of identifying that part of the presentation that you like the least, and rework it.

In addition, the trainer should solicit feedback from participants throughout the day. By doing so, it may be possible to detect issues that can be addressed during the training. At worst, the recommendations made can be incorporated into later iterations of the training.

The Role of Feedback

The trainer runs the risk of simply issuing information, without gaining any feedback from participants until the review form is passed out at the end of the training session. It is essential to ask for questions as soon as the training begins, so that the trainer has an immediate feedback loop regarding what is being covered and the mode of delivery. Depending on the situation, this allows the trainer to adjust the training to better align with the needs of employees. Consider taking the following steps to extract comments from participants:

- Tell the group up-front that questions and comments are expected and appreciated.
- Whenever there is a break between topics, ask for questions and comments.

- Watch participants for puzzled expressions and immediately make an inquiry.
- Be available during breaks to take comments from participants.

When comments are made, paraphrase them. Doing so ensures that the trainer has correctly heard the comment, and also ensures that the entire group understands the discussion.

> **Tip:** A participant's feedback comment may be unrelated to the training materials, and so presents the danger of shifting the conversation off-topic. If so, ask the person to discuss the issue during the next scheduled break.

Dealing with Difficult People

A training participant may engage in disruptive behavior, such as cracking jokes, dominating the discussion, or belittling others. This distracting behavior has a multiplier effect, since it reduces the effectiveness of the training for everyone in the room. Here are several ways to deal with this behavior:

- Stop talking and wait until the person stops his disruptive behavior. Doing so focuses everyone's attention on the individual; the resulting social pressure may have an impact.
- If ground rules were set up at the beginning of the training, remind everyone of those rules. This approach works best when the ground rules were posted where they can be seen by everyone in the room.
- Ask the person to stop. This approach is needed when the person is being highly disruptive, so that any delay in taking action will interfere with the learning experience.
- Call a break, and discuss the person's actions during the break. This approach is more respectful of the individual's standing, since it can be conducted in relative privacy. It can be used when a person may not be aware that his behavior is causing trouble.
- Actively involve the person in the discussion. This approach can work when the underlying reason for the disruptive behavior is that the person feels excluded.

Summary

The main focus of this chapter has been on the high level of preparation needed by a trainer. A high-grade trainer must take a deep interest in the physical and learning environment of session participants. Doing so can make a notable impact on the interest level exhibited by the trainees, which ultimately leads to a better return on investment for the business.

When a training program includes the many suggestions included within this manual, the overall impact on the business will be a very noticeable jump in the return on investment. Once management notices this improvement, expect the demand for training to increase, with managers sponsoring a larger proportion of the training classes being offered. Thus, a well-run training program that ties back to business needs and assists employees through the implementation process is likely to become a significant partner to the management team. As such, trainers will be brought into discussions of strategy and tactics, and their opinions will be valued.

Glossary

E

E-learning. The use of electronic technologies to access training outside of a traditional classroom.

L

Learning objectives. A specification of the desired knowledge or skill of an employee after training has been completed.

P

Payback period. The amount invested in training, divided by the annual cash flows expected as a result of the training.

Pilot training. When a training session is conducted with a small group in advance of rolling out the training to a larger group, to solicit trainee reactions.

R

Return on investment. The amount of return on an investment relative to its cost.

S

Spacing effect. The concept that learning is greater when it is spread out over a period of time.

T

Training. The process of imparting information in order to improve performance.

Index